You, Me and Us

Ideas for activities about ourselves
for pre-key stage 1 children

by

Carole Creary and Gay Wilson

Curriculum Advisers for Primary Science

NIAS

Northamptonshire Inspection and Advisory Service

Introduction

How this book will help

It will:
- give you some understanding of how young children learn science
- provide a bank of simple and enjoyable learning activities
- build a firm foundation for later learning in science
- provide you with necessary background information
- help you to make the most of opportunities for science learning in everyday activities

What is science for the pre-school child?

With very young children, science could be defined as finding out about and making sense of the world around us and our place in it. As well as acquiring knowledge it is also about developing an enquiring and questioning attitude. Children need to be encouraged to develop their own ideas and to express these ideas in words even though at this stage the ideas may not be scientifically correct.

How do children learn science?

Science is a very practical subject and children will learn most by 'doing'. They will learn a great deal through play but this play needs to be directed if the full potential for science learning is to be realised.

They will need encouragement to use all their senses, within the bounds of safety, as they investigate and explore the world around and to talk about what they are doing and what they have found out.

- playing games helps them to become aware of their own bodies
- playing with other children can help them to understand the similarities and differences between people
- exploring and investigating objects and materials helps them realise that their senses can tell them about the world
- helping to prepare food shows that eating and drinking are essential to life

How do we help children learn science?

- by asking questions such as;
  - What do you think?
  - Why do you think that?
  - What if...?
- by encouraging them to question
- by encouraging them to put ideas into words
- by valuing their ideas
- by providing opportunities for children to explore using all their senses
- by helping the child to develop the appropriate language

Making the most of science

Often the opportunity to develop a child's scientific thinking is lost because the potential for science in the activity has not been recognised. Thinking clearly about why we are asking the child to do a particular activity and what is the learning we expect to take place, can be helpful. To this end we have included science learning objectives for each activity in the book.

Where next?

The activities in this book will give children a good foundation for later learning at school, particularly in the Life Processes and Living Things aspect of national curriculum science.

Contents

Activity summary

This side of the page gives a summary of the children's activity to you, the adult. It gives you an idea of the sort of questions that might be raised or the way in which the children's thinking might be guided.

Objectives

This gives you the main learning that is expected from the activity. They help you plan and direct activities with greater purpose.

Breathing

· Put your hand on a friend's chest while they breathe in and out.
· What can you feel?
· What can you hear?
· Let your friend feel you breathing.
· Run round the playground together.
· Feel your chest again.
· What can you feel now?
· What is different?

10

Objectives: To know that we breathe.
To begin to work co-operatively.

· Children should be encouraged to feel and listen to each other breathing normally before running round the playground.
· Note the difference when they are out of breath and breathing harder.

Beware!

· Make sure that children do not have medical conditions which may be aggravated by strenuous exercise.

Extension:
· Introduce the idea that we breathe air
· Discuss the fact that other animals breathe.

You will need:
The children.

This side of the page offers you some extra help or advice and sometimes ideas for extension activities.

Beware!

This warning symbol appears wherever there may be a safety consideration. Children should be taught to work safely and sensibly. Only by encountering hazards in a safe and controlled environment will they learn to do so. More information may be found in "Be Safe!" available from the Association for Science Education, College Lane, Hatfield, Herts. AL 10 9AA. ISBN 0 86357 081 X

You will need:

This gives you a list of all the materials and equipment you will need for the activity

What am I like?

I've got one nose and one mouth but two eyes

- Look at yourself in the mirror.
- What do you see?
- Tell a grown-up or your friend the names of all the things you can see on your face.
- Can you draw a picture of yourself?
- Look at your friends. How are they the same, how are they different?
- Draw your friend.

Objectives: To know that we all have similar features and to note the similarities and differences between them.

- Discuss with the children that we all have eyes, ears, noses, mouths, etc. but we all look different. Why?
- Note that eyes, hair, skin may be different colours.
- Are our faces all the same shape?

Extension:

- Make faces on paper plates using collage materials for features.

You will need:

Mirrors (long if possible),

Objectives: To recognise and name parts of the body.

This activity is a good foundation for the National Curriculum requirement in Key Stage 1, that children should be able to name the main external parts of the body.

Extension:
· Draw the children's attention to the similarities between themselves and others, eg we all have heads, legs, arms, etc.
· Discuss differences, eg eye colour, hair colour, skin colour, shape of nose, etc.

You will need:
The children.

Parts of us

· Do you know the song 'Heads, shoulders, knees and toes'?
· Can you do the actions while you sing?
· Does everyone have a head, shoulders, knees and toes?
· Do you know the names of any other parts of you?

3

You, me and us

• Look at your friends.

• What are they like?

• How are they like you?

• How many things do you all have the same?

• How many things are different?

Objectives: To know that there are similarities and differences in human beings.

• Much of the early work in the Life and Living Processes aspect of the National Curriculum involves close observation and making comparisons, noting similarities and differences in human beings and other species.

• This activity begins to lay foundations for this later work.

• This activity could also provide an opportunity for talking about children with disabilities and how they adapt.

You will need:
The children

4

Objectives: To know that there are similarities and differences between us.
To begin to work co-operatively.

- Children should be encouraged to measure their hands against each other using language such as bigger, smaller, longer, shorter, etc.
- Look carefully at each other's hands. We all have hands but how are they different?

Extension:

- Use a magnifier to look even more closely at hands.
- Look especially at fingernails - a good introduction for talking about the need to wash hands before touching food.

You will need:

Fairly thick paint, tray for paint, paper, soap and water, bowl and towel.

Handy

- Work with a partner.
- Press your open hand against your partner's hand.
- Are your hands the same size?
- Whose hand is bigger?
- Whose is smaller?
- Try with a different partner.
- Is everyone's hand different?
- Make some handprint pictures to show everyone.

Making tracks

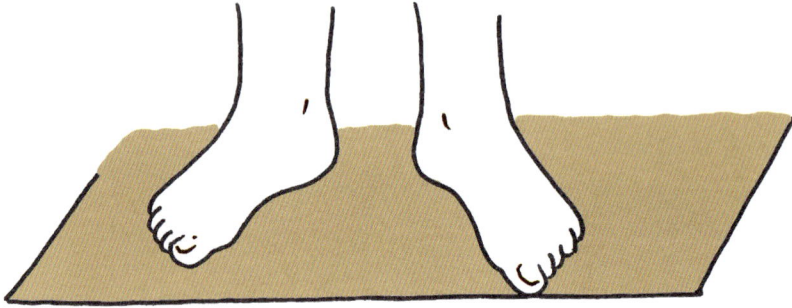

· Take your shoes and socks off.
· Tread carefully in the talcum powder and stand on the black paper.
· Step off carefully without smudging.
· What can you see?
· Compare your footprints with your friend's.
· Are they the same?
· How are they different?
· How many toes have you got?

Objectives: To look closely at feet.
To be able to name some body parts.
To have fun.

· Spray the talcum powder footprints with hair spray to fix them.
· Similar footprints may be made with paint but is much messier!
· Encourage the children to look at the size and shape of the footprints.
· Cut them out and use as non-standard measures.

Extension:

· Does the tallest child have the longest feet?

You will need:

A tray, talcum powder, dark paper, hair spray.

Objectives: To know that our hands are not the same size.

· This activity may be combined with counting practice or use one to one correspondence to find out which hand has picked up most.

· Objects such as wooden beads, clothes pegs, lollysticks or drinking straws make suitable items for picking up.

Extension:

· Try picking up similar items with your toes.

· How are toes different from fingers?

You will need:

Collections of objects such as lollysticks, pegs, beads, marbles, straws etc.

How many can you pick up?

· Look at the things in front of you.

· How many can you pick up in one hand?

· Can you pick up the same number with the other hand?

· How many can your friend pick up?

· Who can pick up most with one hand?

· Can you pick up more of some things than others?

How tall are you?

- Are you and your friends all the same height?

Speech bubble: I think my strip will be longest

- Lie down on a paper ribbon and ask a friend to mark where your head and feet come.
- Cut the ribbon at the marks.
- Write your name on it and decorate it to make it special.
- Compare your strip with your friends.
- Whose strip is longer? Taller?
- Who is the tallest in your group?

Objectives: To know that we are not all the same height.

To know that we grow at different rates.

- Compare the children's heights by standing them back to back, measuring against marks on the wall, etc.
- Line the children up in height order.
- Children may need help in realising that their length on the floor is the same as their height when they stand up.
- Do this activity each term to see how the children are growing.

Extension:

- Are the oldest children the tallest?

You will need:

Paper ribbon (till roll), name cards, crayons, felt tips, sequins, glue, etc.

Objectives: To know about the wide variety of ways in which we can move our bodies.

To learn the names of different movements.

- Discuss the different parts of the body that the children are moving.
- Can they name the various parts?
- Can they name the type of movement?

  Skipping, jumping, running, hopping, rolling, crawling.

Extension:

- Practise stopping, starting and changing direction.
- Play 'Statues'.

You will need:

A large space in which to move safely.

Hop, skip and jump

- Move all about using all the space.
- In how many different ways can you move?
- Which parts of you are you moving?
- Which parts are touching the floor?

Only my toes are on the floor

My hands, my bottom and my feet are on the floor

- Work with a partner to find ways of moving together.

Breathing

- Put your hand on a friend's chest while they breathe in and out.
- What can you feel?
- What can you hear?
- Let your friend feel you breathing.
- Run round the playground together.
- Feel your chest again.
- What can you feel now?
- What is different?

Objectives: To know that we breathe.
To begin to work co-operatively.

- Children should be encouraged to feel and listen to each other breathing normally before running round the playground.
- Note the difference when they are out of breath and breathing harder.

Beware!

- Make sure that children do not have medical conditions which may be aggravated by strenuous exercise.

Extension:

- Introduce the idea that we breathe air
- Discuss the fact that other animals breathe.

You will need:

The children.

Objectives: To know that we breathe in and out.
To work with a partner.

· To make a breathing tube remove both ends from a Smartie tube and fix a small streamer firmly to one end.

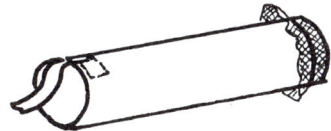

Beware!

· Make sure the streamer is firmly fixed so that children cannot accidentally inhale it. A small piece of net may be fastened over the mouth end for extra safety.

You will need:

Empty Smartie tube or similar, tissue paper, sellotape, scissors, net, elastic band.

Breathe and blow

· Make a breathing tube.
· Work with a partner.
· Hold your tube to your lips.
· Breathe in and out hard through your mouth.

· What is happening to the little streamer?
· What can your partner see?
· Breathe gently. What do you notice now?

Eat, drink and be merry

Ice-cream is my favourite but I mustn't eat too much!

I do like apples as well

- Think of some of your favourite foods.
- Why do you think we need to eat and drink?
- Are some foods better for us than others?
- Do we always like the things that are good for us?
- Make a model of your favourite meal on a paper plate.

Objectives: To know that we need food and water to stay alive.

- Ask children what they feel like when they are hungry.
- How do they feel after they have eaten?
- Discuss the need for food and drink.
- What would happen if we didn't eat or drink?
- Discuss in simple terms why some foods are better for us than others, eg too many sweet things affect our teeth.

Extension

- When is the best time to eat sweet things?
- What should we do after eating them?

You will need:

Paper plates, plastic food or materials for making pretend food, paint, glue.

Objectives: To know that medicines can help to make us better when we are ill.
To know the difference between medicines and sweets.

· Talk about the medicines that some children may need to take regularly.

· Explain that we should never take anything from someone we don't know.

· Emphasise that they should never eat any "sweets" they might find.

· Discuss the difference between medicine bottles and sweet packets.

· Help the children to identify and sort different bottles and packages.

You will need:
Empty pill and medicine bottles, empty sweet packets, tubes, boxes, etc.

When is it good for us?

· Does a grown up sometimes give you medicine?

· Why and what for?

· What is the difference between medicine and sweets?

· Can you sort out the things you may eat from the things you should only eat or drink if a grown up says so?

Yum or yuk!!

· You may taste each of the foods in front of you.

· What do they each taste like?

· Do you like them all?

· Can you sort them into yuk or yum sets?

I don't like this. It's too sour

I wonder if you can change the taste of things

· Do your friends like the same foods as you?

· Which part of your body do you use for tasting things?

Objectives: To know that we taste things in our mouths.

To appreciate that there are different tastes.

· Use foods such as fruits including lemon or grapefruit, breads, biscuits, raw vegetables, cereals, etc.

· Children should always be warned of the dangers of tasting unknown substances.

· Discuss how the texture of food might affect our likes or dislikes.

· Link with "Vegetable soup" from "All sorts of stuff" in this series.

· Blindfold the children and repeat the activity to see if the children can identify the foods.

You will need:

A variety of different foods.

Objectives: To know that we can feel things when we touch them.

To know that there are different textures.

To develop descriptive language.

Sensory activities should be kept simple at this stage.

Children need to be made aware that our whole body is sensitive to touch and not just our fingers.

Encourage the children to develop the appropriate language such as rough, smooth, cold, warm, silky, smooth, etc.

You will need:

A variety of objects or materials of different textures.

Touch and feel

· Hold your friend's hand. Can you feel it?

· Sit quietly on the floor. Can you feel it?

· Close your eyes and ask your friend to touch you on different parts of your body. Can you feel it?

This is hard and cold. I think it is a stone.

· Feel all the things in front of you.

· Tell someone what they feel like.

· Hide them in a feely bag and try to guess which one you are feeling.

Hear, hear!

- Listen carefully to the sounds all around you. What can you hear?
- Which part of your body do you use to hear with?

If my ears are covered, I can't hear very well.

- Ask a friend to bang gently on a drum.
- Listen carefully.
- Put your hands over your ears or put some headphones on.
- What difference does it make?
- What happens if they bang louder?

Objectives: To know that we hear with our ears.

To know that there are different sounds and different sources of sound.

- Encourage children to look closely at each other's ears.
- Draw or paint portraits making sure that ears are included.
- Compare the shape of our ears with that of other animals.
- Can we move our ears like them?
- Why do they move their ears?
- Make headbands with ears for role play.

You will need:

Drum and beater, head phones or ear protectors.

Objectives: To know that we see with our eyes.
To know that we need to take
special care of our eyes.

- Children need to be aware that we see with our eyes, smell with our noses, etc., in preparation for understanding that our senses enable us to find out about the world.
- Discuss the dangers of throwing sand into other's eyes, poking, etc.
- Why do some people need to wear spectacles?
- How do people who can't see get about, read, write, etc.

You will need:
Mirrors, drawing materials.

Look and see

- Look around you. What can you see?
- Close your eyes. What can you see now?
- Can you see in the dark?
- Look at your eyes in a mirror.
- Can you see the different parts?
- Look at your friend's eyes. Are they the same as yours? How are they different?
- Can you draw a picture of your eyes?

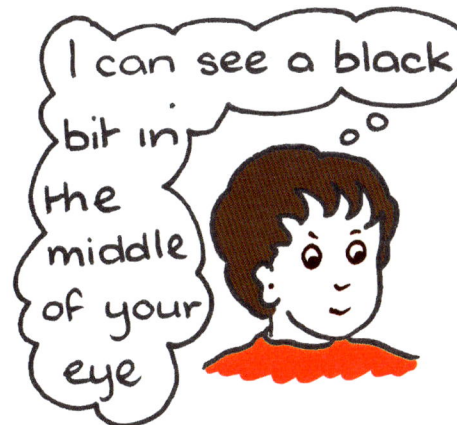

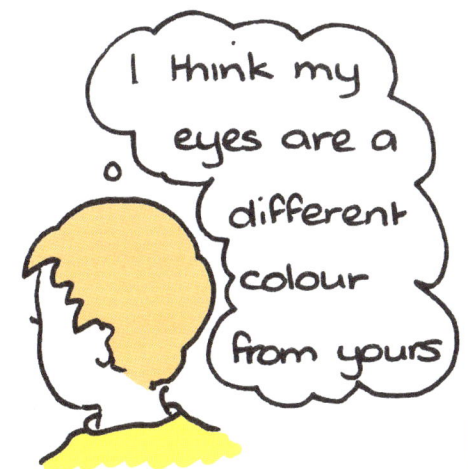

I can see a black bit in the middle of your eye

I think my eyes are a different colour from yours

Sniffy

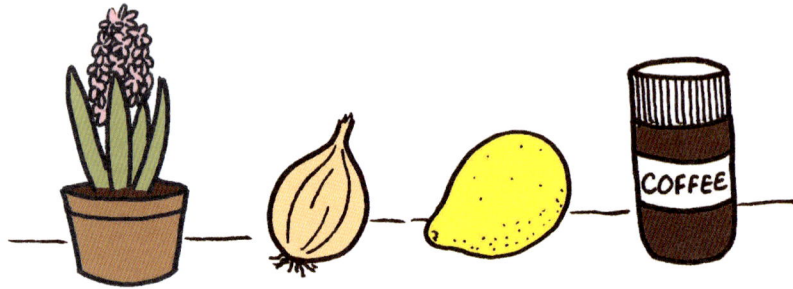

- Choose something from the smelly collection.
- What does the smell remind you of?
- Which part of your body do you use to smell with?
- Do you like all the smells on the table?
- Which is your favourite?
- Does everyone like the same one?
- Which smells don't you like?

Objectives: To know that we smell things with our noses.
To know that there are different smells.

- Encourage children to try and describe different smells although this is difficult.
- Do not include fine powders (eg. ground spices) at this stage in case children sniff with too much enthusiasm!
- Warn children to take care if sniffing unknown substances.
- Look at noses. Are they all the same?
- Do all animals have noses?

Beware!

You will need:
A variety of items with distinctive smells.

Objectives: To make children aware of the need for personal hygiene.

To know that hygiene is important to health.

- Make a collection of things we use to help with personal hygiene, eg soap, flannel, towel, toothpaste, toothbrush, empty containers of bathfoam, shampoo, etc.
- Discuss how these are used to help us keep clean.
- Talk about the importance of washing hands after using the toilet.
- Have a dolly's bathtime and washday.
- Invite the dental hygienist in to talk.

You will need:

A collection of personal hygiene aids.

Keeping clean

If I keep my eyes closed tight, the soap won't go in

I like it when my hair is clean and shiny

- How do you keep clean?
- Look at all the things in the "Keeping clean" collection.
- What are they all used for?
- Which do you use everyday?
- Why?
- Why is it important for us to keep ourselves clean?
- Paint a picture of you cleaning your teeth or having a bath.

Wash your hands!

> I thought my hands were clean!
>
> Where did all that dirt come from?

- Dip your hands in some clean water.
- Now wipe your hands on a clean white cloth or towel.
- Look carefully at the towel.
- Where has all that dirt come from?
- What might happen if that dirt gets on to your food?
- Now wash your hands properly with soap and water.

Objectives: To know that our hands get dirty.
To know that we cannot always see the dirt.
To know that this dirt could make us ill if it gets on our food.

- Children will need to be introduced to the idea that there are things too small to be seen.
- Discuss why we need to wash our hands before we eat or handle food.
- Re-inforce the rules of hygiene during cookery activities.
- Do this activity after a messy activity or after playtime.

You will need:

A bowl of clean water, clean white cloth or towel.

Objectives: To know that we feel uncomfortable if we are too hot.

To know that our choice of clothes can help keep us cool.

- Encourage the children to talk about how they feel if they get too hot.
- Have they looked in a mirror after running about on a hot day?
- Why is their hair all wet? Why is their face red?
- Ask the children for their ideas about why this happens.
- Introduce the idea that cool drinks are important when it is very hot.

You will need:

A dressing up box with a wide variety of clothes.

Keeping cool

I must remember to wear my hat if the sun is hot

- Pretend that it is a very hot day.
- Choose some clothes from the dressing up box to wear on a hot day.
- Why is it important to wear a hat if the sun is very hot?
- Why do we need to put sun cream on when we go out in the sun?

Keeping warm

- Pretend that it is a very cold day.
- Look in the dressing up box.
- Which clothes would you wear to keep yourself warm?
- Put them on.
- Can you dress yourself?

I feel lovely and warm now

.... but I wouldn't want to wear these on a hot day!

Objectives: To know that we need to keep our bodies warm.
To know that clothes can help to do this.

- Encourage children to talk about what it feels like to be cold.
- Have they ever noticed goose pimples on their skin?
- What happens when they shiver?
- What can we do to keep ourselves warm?
- Encourage the children to talk about their ideas for doing this.
- Introduce the idea that hot food or drink can also help.

You will need:

A dressing up box with warm clothes, cool clothes and waterproof clothing.

Objectives: To know that waterproof clothes will help to keep us dry.

- Talk about why we need to keep dry.
- Use scraps of fabric to investigate which will soak up water and which will not.
- Stretch some materials over a container and pour water over it to find out which let water through.
- Introduce vocabulary such as wet, dry, waterproof, soaking, etc.
- Use a watering can with a fine rose to pour water onto an umbrella. Observe what happens.

You will need:

A wide selection of clothes, an umbrella, watering can, scraps of fabric, plastic sheet.

Keeping dry

- Look at the clothes in the dressing-up box.
- Pretend that it is raining.
- Which clothes would you wear to keep you dry?
- What else could help to keep the rain off you?

I could splash through the puddles in my wellingtons

A lovely smile

- Look in a mirror.
- Give a lovely big smile.
- Look carefully at your teeth.

The teeth at the back are flat on top

Some teeth are smaller than others

- Are they all the same?
- Why do we need to clean them?
- Where might food get caught?
- Draw a picture of your lovely smile.
- Do you know anyone who has lost some teeth?

Objectives: To know that we need to look after our teeth.

- The sooner children begin to understand the need to take care of their teeth the better.
- Discuss with children why too many sweets are bad for our teeth.
- What other things might be harmful?
- Which foods are good for our teeth and gums?
- Invite the dental health visitor to talk to the children.
- Talk about a visit to the dentist. What happens? Why do we need to go?

You will need:

Examples of toothbrushes, toothpaste, etc.

Objectives: To know that babies grow into children who in turn grow into adults.

- Make a collection of baby pictures.
- Discuss with the children the things that babies are able to do.
- Compare with what they are able to do now.

Extension:
- Invite a new baby in and compare the size of hands and feet.
- Talk about the way we have to care for new babies.

You will need:
A collection of pictures of babies, especially the children as babies.

Bye Baby Bunting

- Look at a photograph of yourself when you were a baby.
- How have you changed?
- Can you guess which baby picture belongs to which of your friends?
- Look at some pictures of grown-ups when they were babies.
- Do you recognise them?
- How have they changed?

Poems

This little piggy went to market
    This Little Puffin   ISBN 14 030300 6

Noses
Jeremiah
Bedtime
    Young Puffin Book of Verse   ISBN 0 14030 410 X

What's the matter with Mary Jane?
    A A Milne

When we were very young
    Mammouth   ISBN 07497 0209 5

Songs

If you're happy and you know it
    Apusskidu A & C Black   ISBN 0 7136 1553 2

Heads and shoulders, knees and toes
Looby Loo
Miss Polly had a dolly
Do your ears hang low?
Put your finger on your head
    Okki-Tokki-Unga A & C Black   ISBN 0 7136 4078 2

Here we go round the mulberry bush
    Sing Hey Diddle Diddle A & C Black   ISBN 0 7136 2334 9

Stories

Stories are often a good way of introducing science activities. Below are a few suggestions of stories that will help introduce or reinforce work on ourselves.

Bouncing   ISBN 0 7445 2513 6
Hiding   0 7445 3249 3
Chatting   0 7445 3248 5
Giving   0 7445 2512 8
    Shirley Hughes
    Published by Walker Books

All about Alice   0 7445 3164 0
    Penny Dale
    Published by Walker Books

I can't sleep
    Philippe Dupasquier
    Published by Walker Books   ISBN 0 7445 2061 4

Little Red Riding Hood
    Oxford University Press   ISBN 0 19 279794 8

Funny Bones stories

Ourselves - essential background knowledge

The senses

Touch - Nerve endings in the skin allow us to feel with any part of our bodies but some areas, such as the finger tips, have more nerve endings and are therefore more sensitive.

Hearing - Our ears are sensitive to sounds which cause the ear drum, the tiny bones in the middle ear and the fluid in the inner ear to vibrate, passing messages via the auditory nerve to the brain.

Sight - Light is reflected from objects. This light enters the eye through the pupil and messages are passed via sensitive cells in the retina to the optic nerve and thence to the brain.

Smell - Receptors in the nose detect small particles in the air and pass the appropriate messages to the olfactory nerve.

Taste - The tongue is covered with taste buds. Specific buds in different areas respond to different tastes such as sweet, sour, salty and bitter. Smell and taste are closely linked which is why we cannot taste or smell anything when we have a bad cold.

All sensory information is processed and decoded by the brain which enables us to make sense of the world around us.

The heart and circulation

The heart is a pump which circulates blood round the body. As the blood is pumped through the lungs, waste gases are exchanged for oxygen. It then returns to the heart and is pumped to all parts of the body. The blood delivers oxygen and nutrients and waste products are collected and carried to organs such as the liver and kidneys for elimination.

The skeleton and muscles

We are able to stand upright and move as we do because we have a skeleton and muscles. The skeleton provides a frame to which muscles are attached and these muscles, usually working in pairs, enable us to move.

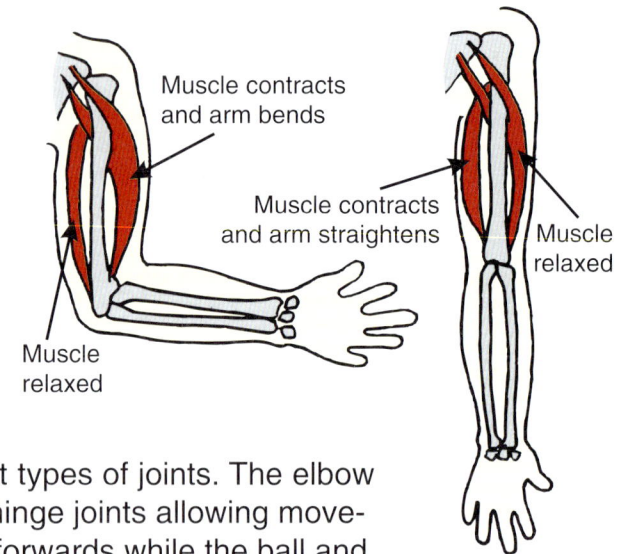

Muscle contracts and arm bends

Muscle contracts and arm straightens

Muscle relaxed

Muscle relaxed

We also have different types of joints. The elbow and knee are simple hinge joints allowing movement backwards and forwards while the ball and socket joints at shoulder and hip allow and much wider range of movement. The wrist and ankle joints are made up of many small bones which gives a much more complex range of movement.